DRAG QUEEN PREACHER

Drag Queen Preacher

R.R. Tavárez

the pilgrim press

The Pilgrim Press
1300 East 9th Street
Cleveland, Ohio 44114

thepilgrimpress.com

Library of Congress cataloging-in-publication data on file.
LCCN: 2024949981

ISBN 978-0-8298-0570-3 (paper)
ISBN 978-0-8298-1157-5 (ebook)

Typeset in Rafaella and Adobe Caslon.

Printed in the United States of America on acid-free paper.

Contents

For those who left the Church to find God.

Photo credit: Hwa Jeen Na

Photo credit: Amanda Adams

Foreword

¡Borinquen!, nombre al pensiamento grato
como el Recuerdo de un amor profundo,
bello Jardin, de América el ornato.
siendo el jardin América del mundo.
—Jose Gautier Benitz, "¡Puerto Rico!"

R.R. Tavárez's volume *Drag Queen Preacher* is a stunning, comprehensive spiritual journey. His family embodies their Puerto Rican and Dominican heritage of dance and song in the garden of his homeland, and in coming to the mainland they find themselves aliens in a strange land full of violence and bigotry, yet he rises to confront the rage and sorrow he sees all about him. The testimonies to his growth to a proud queer Latino, a drag queen pastor sharing his many identities with those still unsure of themselves and their place in this life, lead to his life as an activist living a life of service to those ashamed and in need, unaware of the value of their lives and identities.

These are "unchained words" with many points of reference, the multiple identities of a complicated spirit loving his family and heritage, as seen in his poems for his Abuela and Abuelita, honoring them as forerunners to his own life and love. Tavárez uses his poetry as touchstones to move those who come to this book, that they too may awaken to the many kindnesses one may share in spite of poverty and racism, the awareness of love as the rose in a new dawn with petals opening to the beauty of living well.

Indeed, this book is a major contribution to LGBTQ+ literature and the literature of drag in performance, as well as the spirituality of religious help for those in real need. Tavárez's work is a guide through these horrors to find fulfillment and awareness. Each section of the book opens doors to new revelations despite setbacks, with the ensuing determination to find love and the awareness to share it with others. Thus, "cross the chasm of lies / On this side, you will have / less anger, less fear / You will have much more joy."

David Cope
January 6, 2025

Preface

Beloved,

I am one person. But I am not one thing.

I am a drag queen. I am a seminary-trained pastor.

I am the aftermath of Spanish colonizers. I am the resilience of African slaves.

I am Dominican. I am Puerto Rican.

I am part of an immigrant family. I am a citizen of the United States.

I am Brooklyn-born. I am Grand Rapids-raised.

I am a skilled administrator. I am an unsatisfied artist.

I am lost. I am found.

I am romantic. I am realistic.

I am wounded. I am healed.

I am all these words and yet my story is still being written.

On more than one occasion I have been encouraged to share my personal unfolding story. As a would-be casualty of culture wars and a survivor of religious abuse, certain colleagues have told me that I've experienced more pain and accomplishment in my young tenure as a nonwhite, openly gay pastor than most minsters have in their lifetime. Through workshops, lectures, sermons, and yes, even on the mic as a drag queen, I've shared pieces of my life's journey. I have affirmed many an audience that we, as humans, are so much more than a single identity, and that it's more than possible to be gay and a faithful Christian. To the credit of my colleagues, I know this message can go so much further in writing.

Being a writer has been one of my life's great ambitions for as long as I can remember. As a youth I began by privately writing children's stories and superhero tales. In early college I played with short stories. Eventually I moved into essays and articles related to my profession. Between engaging in all these mediums, poetry has consistently drawn me to the written page. And thus, it's in this first collection of poetry that I bring to you my unfolding story, and beloved, I hope it helps you see your own story in a new light.

This collection of poetry has been curated into four sections. Los Espíritus invites you to see again the ghostly visions that shape our present. Aire is the spiral of joy we enter when we decide to become who we are meant to be. Lo Que Se Pierde is what we lose in the process of becoming. Cuerpos de Alabanza are the praises we sing, not when everything is okay, but when we accept that which wc arc.

In each section, you will see me paying homage to the heritage I hold through my paternal and maternal grandmothers, Abuela and Abuelita respectively. You will read dramatized journal entries. You will witness the barrier between sacred and secular being removed. You follow a gay man longing for love, a minister walking on the fringes of society and a drag queen moving from rage to empowerment. You will find prayers, doubts, liturgies, the embracing of sexuality, Spanish verbs, and battles against racism and bigotry.

May your growth be nurtured here. May you find camaraderie and belonging. For the skeptics, may you be open to the possibility of faith through a new lens. For the complacent, may your hearts be moved to justice. But what I truly hope for all of us is that you discover within these words a part of yourself and our shared human experience.

Con Amor,

Rev. R.R. Tavárez

Book One:
Los Espiritus

Garden

Meet me in the garden
Where I dig my knees
Into the dirt
Prayin'
Where my brow sweat
Falls to the earth
That waits with its mouth
Open
Hopin'
To see
The children of God
Revealed

They told me
I could be anything
So, I choose
To be
Me

They told me
I could be everything
But I choose
To be
Free

They handed me
A shovel
Asked me if I wouldn't change my mind

Silence

They told me git to diggin'
Errbody watchin'
Errbody waitin' for a revolution
Errbody take to fallin'
Asleep

Silence

But not me
I am getting ready to be planted
And if this queer body has to die
Then so be it

All morning I threw dirt over my shoulder
Hauled then, a few rocks, a boulder
Til I could stand waist deep in their sin

Did it all day
Til the sun faded its rays
Tilled til I was ready to lay me down
To become the garden.

Full of tiger lilies and an oak tree that will shade
The hunger of a generation
Yet to be created

So here I pray
As you walk away
Talking about my potential to grow

And now I lay
Cross my arms over my chest
Ready for this blessed rest
But eyes always
Wide open

Silence

I wait

Silence

Will anyone bury me?
Then the earth shudders
I hear the voice

"Not yet."

Aquí en Michigan

Hace calor
Abuelita says
We find her in the kitchen of the apartment
Wearing nothing but a bra and a half slip
¡Mami! Tia gasps
I laugh, and laugh, and laugh
Six and sixty-years-old
Adjusting to this new place
The white people keep telling us
It's not the heat
It's the humidity that'll kill ya
Abuelita doesn't know the difference
Leaning over the stove to stir a pot of pinto beans

The Weston apartments are home for Abuelita
Tia too
They are downtown
Or uptown
Depending on who you ask
I ask Tia
Why does the elevator smell like pee?
Every time we go up and down

Sometimes she doesn't answer
Once she points at a puddle in the back corner
And I've never felt more trapped
As we wait for the door to open again

We left *Nueva York* for this place
Grand Rapids. Michigan.
More opportunities, Tia explains
We ignore the boarded-up buildings
And meander toward what she calls *la plaza*
The summer flows from the sidewalk
The last summer before I start first grade. 1991.

Did you go to school Tia?
In Puerto Rico?
She takes my hand and tells me about walking through
Butterfly fields on her way home from class
Her and her friends, climbing mango trees

It's time to go home for dinner
This new home
The elevator climbs up, Abuelita greets us
Arroz y habichuelas
There is a twinkle in her green eyes
She tells me to bless the food
English is okay, she says
But I pray in Spanish. And God listens.

Please, Open the Doors

I feel my dignity tear away
With every car driving
On Buchanan Avenue
To whatever place their drivers call work
Shame fills my throat
I have no name
For what crawls the perimeter of my belly
Standing outside in the food pantry line
At Mount Olivet Church

Please, open the doors
I think at the church
And please, don't look at me
I think at the drivers
Likely no one takes much notice
Of this colored boy
Glued to his mother's skirt
Just another line of Hispanic immigrants
Hoping for milk and honey
Collecting cornflakes and cranberry sauce instead

Succession

In seventh grade, Mr. Bow told me
Poems don't always have to rhyme

He gave me Langston Hughes
W.E.B. Du Bois
Richard Wright

No Afro-Latinos in the curriculum
But I could see it
The horizon

My Black teacher pointed to the promised land and
  said
Don't let the rules meant to scare you get in your way
I concluded my words should be
My words must be
Unchained

The walls of Jericho and religion came falling
As I furiously started screaming
On every page I could get my pencil to reach

Family Photos, Fotos Familiares

Sit with me, *mis hermanas*
How long has it been?

We could write on the dust collected on this photo album

Turn with me, *las historias*
Black and white photos, now yellow bordered

They fall free, plastic pages having lost their cling

They came a long way, *de la isla*
To Long Island, New York

Retrace the barefoot journey, fresh fruit, rain and well water

We are foreigners there, *somos extranjeros aquí*
We add a new island, Michigan, to the story

Hijos, encontramos lucha. Together, *encontramos fuerza.*

Will You Be There?

Will you be there?
At the river
As it rolls softly
Over my toes
That timidly tickle
The colored pebbles
In the shallows
Lapping among the reeds

Will you be there?
When the cold
Nibbles at my skin
Sending goosebumps
Everywhere
And the water
Begins to dance between my legs
Pulling me into its sway
When I finally dare to feel the spirit
At my knees
As I hold my skirt up
To keep the fabric dry

Will you be there?
When I'm gasping
The currents swelling
Around my throat
As I come to the depth
That I can no longer ford
Knowing that air
Belongs to the world
And I to the river
That fills my ears
With my name
A single exasperated note

Will you be there?
As I hold my breath
And swim and push
My own mind
To believe that a river
Emanating from this temple
Can unsalt the sea
And reckon with a world unseen
A time untold
A heart unyielding
To settle for yellow suns
That are meant to glow red
And I am sunken
Among the echoes
That formed me

For this humble river
Has become
The mighty Jordan of old
The Pishon
The Gihon
The Euphrates
The Tigris
And the Nile
Fish filled
Rebirthing this earth
Long been dusty
With faded drumbeats
Of warring tribes
Refreshing vigor
This river
Now draws me
To the other side

Will you be there?
On the other side?
As I am brought forth
As a stranger
Laughing
The ridiculous notion
Of a plunge
Dripping off my shoulders
Now standing and wringing my hair
Clearing the water from my eyelashes
Looking for a friend

Progeny

Hablame en Español
Papi says
Lying in bed
Awake
Eyes shut
Super cansado
Still in his work uniform
And so, I try over and over
And so, he corrects the long and short use of my vowels
Until I sound less like an *Americano*
And more like him
A survivor
In whom he is well pleased

Mami is downstairs
Living in the rhythm of
Rice and beans
Rice and beans
Rice and beans
Rice and on Sundays
Yuca and *plátano majado*
Until the rhythm blesses my soul too

Giving me the *ganas* to press on
In the torrents
Written to erase
My will.

Modern History

So, are you Black? Or Hispanic?

Yes, stupid questions do exist in abundance
Around these parts

Because they imagine the world begins at Plymouth
  Rock
As if Genesis opens with, let there be white

Actually, ma'am
Columbus trafficked African slaves to Hispaniola
Before your country was even a concept

So, is that something you're proud of?

Jesus and other expletives

No, but to answer your earlier question
Please go read a book

Photo credit: Hwa Jeen Na

My Sister Arrested in Burton Heights

What is the charge?
Resisting arrest.
But what was the officer arresting her for?
Resisting arrest.
But what was the crime that made him arrest her?
That's it. Resisting arrest.
You're telling me that he arrested her
For resisting arrest.
Are they really allowed to do that?

-My sister speaks
I'm walking home
The police officer tells me
Approach his car
It is getting dark
He is a man
I am a woman
I don't feel safe
I am a woman alone
I don't feel safe

What do you want?
Come to the car
Have I done something wrong?
Come to the car
Am I being detained?
Come to the car
No

I turn to leave
He opens his car door
He runs to me
I scream
He tackles me
I scream
I scream
I scream

Do you see these
Bruises
This is where he hit me
Pinned me down
He never told me
What did he want?

But what was the officer arresting her for?
Walking while Black.
But what was the crime that made him arrest her?
That's it. And being a woman.
In a poor immigrant neighborhood
You're telling me that he arrested her
Because he thought she was vulnerable
Are they really allowed to do that?

Primary Language

Tu eres Americano
You are American

Yo soy puertorriqueña
I am Puerto Rican

It's no use arguing
How do I explain to Abuelita how they see me?
That I will never be American enough
On the playground
In the classroom
At the children's ministry of the Baptist church

She lays back in her bed
Into a groove that has been shaped
By diabetes, stomach ulcers
I sit back and replay the conversations

What is your primary language?
Spanish
No, what language do you speak at home?
Español
Wow, but you're so articulate
I keep my mouth tight
You're such a smart boy

Yes, but they don't know
How I study the way white men speak
On the video cassettes Papi brings home
I memorize their posture
Diminish my accent
Pretend to be a president, a judge,
A man in a suit, with his own briefcase
Hoping not to be dismissed as just
Another immigrant boy
Rewind and play. Rewind and play.

So, you're bilingual?
Yes. Spanish and English.
That will help you much in the future.
Si, lo sé
Yes. I know

Tributary
(A Eulogy for Tim Porter)

I carry you
And you are weightless

I lay you
On your side
My arms release you
To the tributary
That is my bed

I watch you
Your knees come to
Your sternum
Creating a whirlpool of blue sheets
Against watery gray reflections
For gray is the sky
Even if you are now glorious
As the sea pulls
We separate
Both entering new depths
Full of water

You go. I drift
You float. I dream
You make your petition. I surrender
You take my plenty. I require
Both of us to break
And now. I know

It takes more strength
To release a single tear
Than to hold back the ocean

Personal Dissonance

I freed her from the wardrobe
But not yet the boy

I can't wear that mom
Eliminating all the color
Only when his boys make fun of him
Dude, is your favorite color gray?
Does he add some back
Brown and black
To his palette
It was only pink
He was trying to avoid
And no patterns
Stay solid

Don't walk like that
Men don't walk like that
What does that mean?
The boy doesn't know
So he teaches himself
Tighten your stride
Act like you have weight

Shackles at your ankles
To keep you from floating too high
Stay low boy
Stay low

And somehow yet
The whole block expects you to run
Be ready boy to sprint and tackle
Because if you're aggressive first
Then you won't be taken second
Not for a second
Run headfirst into the locker
Like a bull at the wave of a flag
Crash into the world
They won't fight you
If you make them more afraid of you
Than you are of yourself
Stay scared

But not yet the boy
It's too late for me he says
As if centuries have passed
As if talking to the love of his life
In some action movie where a hero has to die
But we are speaking to ourselves
Boy take my hand. I'm not leaving you behind

Sock Drawer

In this game I call laundry
I find relics in my sock drawer
Looking for a match for this fuzzy purple sock

Look.
Spare buttons in a hand painted zipper bag
My nephew gave me this bag
He was a child then
I was too, I say
What should I do with these now
Buttons to shirts that I've outgrown
Dropped them off to the Goodwill store
When was that?

There are bits of a broken watch
It used to be my favorite thing
I sure thought I was somebody
With that gold tone watch
It snapped one time mid conversation
And cost more to fix than it was worth

Forgot about the sex gimmicks in here...
Did I ever even use this?
I would remember that
Right?

My God.
I have been looking for these makeup wipes
And look at all these gift cards
For places I never go

When did these briefs get back here?

And now I'm sorting the whole damn thing
It's beyond reasonable
Treasures are deposited in the bathroom trash
And I'm questioning everything

Did these coupons expire?
What happened to the label on this tiny bottle?
Is it lotion or shampoo?
When the fuck did I get so many ankle socks?

Why don't I wear dress socks anymore?
Why don't I have places to wear these socks?
When did I stop wearing dress shoes?
How come I don't go to church anymore?
When did they stop inviting me to dinner?

How come we don't eat together at Christmas?
How come I don't care?
And we eat alone. But that's okay.
Is that okay?
I'm not okay.
I'll be okay.
I'll be okay.

I'll be...
There it is. Stupid sock.

Photo credit: Alex Flynn

Passover

(The Pride Flag)

This flag is ferocious
Much too wild for a single household
Invite the outcasts to shelter with you this evening
Take hyssop and dip it in the colors
Streak it across your every door frame
Let it melt into your hands

Why must you wave that thing in our faces?
Nobody wants to see that all the time
They say

This flag is progress
This flag is deliverance
This flag is the outcry for safety
Put it in the sanctuary
Hang it in the windows
Make it a constellation guide

Until the night passes
Until the pestilence of violence
Passes over us

Thirst

I laid my head down in the desert, my pillow
Searching for memories
Finding only thirst
For what you said we would do

Sed

Acosté mi cabeza en el desierto, mi almohada
Buscando recuerdos
Encontrando solo sed
Por lo que dijiste que haríamos

Ashes

You were in my dreams last night
Cliché but true
You whispered to me
In a shrouded room
Then, you lingered
All the living day with me
Strange
The things we remember
Like the way I can see you one year ago
It's Ash Wednesday
You sit at a front row table
Drinking in
Every word within
An ancient text
That calls out today
Speaking both our names

Across a Northern Border

I traveled all the way to Canada
To relearn the art
Of not being on guard
Of not fighting for my right to exist
To relearn what it's like to feel sad for my experience
Without feeling threatened for my existence
To relearn what it's like to feel free
Enough to cry

I rented a basement apartment
Brant Street in downtown Burlington
And after a five-hour drive, three hundred thirty miles
Three days of rest
I said to myself
I'm going to miss him
Knowing I had to go back
I cried for me

Mirror Talk

I flinched in the mirror
But his expression didn't change
He said to me

Perhaps this world wasn't meant for us
But I'm here now. So are you.
In the fleeting moments
Often just once a day
I have enough life to believe
We can shape the world
For people like us
That is the moment
Where we live as one

Lottery

I play the lottery
Usually the Powerball
They tell me it's a sin
That I should pray
Instead for prosperity
I play the numbers anyway
Numbers on rotation
Gotta mix it up, right?
I'm sure God understands

Because my prayers remain constant.

11. 19.
My best friend's birthday. RIP
May I live up to the laugh he left
Echoes I long to hear
Standing at the mouth of this cave

May I make you proud.

I choose the age of my now best friend
I never say that number out loud

It's nobody's business but his own
Just like everything he's gone through

Lord, give him peace.

I choose number 1 sometimes
For the Lord our God is 1

That I might know him.

And sometimes 3
Not for the trinity
But for March
A prayer for Spring

Give us a bit of heaven on this earth.

58 or
64 or
32

Come on God, I need this bread!

7 is so overdone. I never pick 7
But 27, I play for *la patria*
Mi Republica Dominicana

A greeting to my ancestors.

I alternate between 15 and 16
One of them feels right
Fifty percent of the time

Give me wisdom when I do know the right choice
and would choose otherwise.

The most I've ever won?
4 dollars. Let's play 4 today
I'll pay off my student loans
And live the life God has wanted
For me. All along

Life and life abundantly for us with only a ticket in
our pockets.

For J.D. Nixon

Mari and I visit
The Grand River
A few days after you died
It may have been a couple of weeks
The timeline never makes sense
In retrospect, nothing
Ever makes any sense

But we are there
Trudging through glacial temps
The fresh snow is fiercely white
Even after Mari leaves a trail
Footprints on the path
We are pioneering

She looks so vulnerable
Reddish, brownish, grayish hair
Tucked in the hood of her puffer coat
Walking to the water

Can you imagine? You said
What would happen to Mari
If something happened to me
And we talked about battles
Contemporary history
Of cancer, surgeries, nightmares
Of heart problems, fatigue, and
Difficulty breathing
Of holding hands, friendship, and faith

She won't be alone. I said
And neither will you

What Does God Look Like?

God looks like my Puerto Rican *abuelita*
Gray hair. Tied high
Green irises. Lazy eye
A lady. *Una doña*
Poor and humble
Trigueña
Commanding respect
Offering cheese and saltines at every visit

This is who Moses sees on the mountain
Making his face go wild
This is who Elijah leaves in a rush to find
Riding a chariot of fire to paradise, forgetting first
to die
And this is who I see
When I close my eyes

Woman of a thousand strengths
She rubs me down with healing water
On the summer days I fall asleep on her couch
She reads the Psalms over me in broken sentences
Because she taught herself to read

And wants me to believe in something
None of us can afford to purchase

This is who I see
When I close my eyes
When I search for the power of the divine

And you, who do you see?

Recipe

Abuelita never learned to read
So mom never learned to write
Her recipes

How do I make the pinto beans?

You just do it, she says
Watch how I consult the ancestors
With sprinkles of salt and boiling water
Tomato paste and sofrito
Cilantro, onion, garlic,
Green pepper

But you are not using measurements
How will I know what to do?

Ay mijo. My son
Use your tongue. Taste and trust
What you carry in your bones

The Remaining

There is a wall.
There is a wall I'd like to see someday.
A wall in Jerusalem.
A wall, which I'd like to see
while holding hands with my sisters and
standing next to my father.

You see,
my father,
the pastor,
used to tell me stories.
Told me Bible stories out of Leviticus, Numbers and
  Deuteronomy
and his fascination of ancient and modern-day
Jewish culture bled into
his story telling.

And he told me about this wall
in Jerusalem.
A wall that was once part of a temple,
where now people go to pray.

It's called the Western Wall.
It's called the Wailing Wall.
Perhaps you've seen this wall.
Maybe in pictures?

In its hey-day it measured over
one thousand
five hundred feet
in length.
Today,
it's under
two hundred feet long
that ancient wall.
It stands somewhat alone in a kind of courtyard,
holding on to its large un-climbable stones.

The wall's bleached beige crevices are crammed with
prayers,
some of which are on paper.
The rest, spoken verbally,
are captured in the essence of its bricks.

And the people.
They come from the east and the west.
And so do the prayers they bring.
Arriving 24 hours a day.
From the rising of the sun,
to the setting of the same.

The women stand in one corner
and the men in the rest.
In the presence of holiness.
With a never ending, back bending motion.
The last
remaining
portions of God's ancient temple.
No one knows when it began.
This tradition of offering prayers here.
But this portion cannot be destroyed.
The Shekhinah resides.
Thus, praying here is like praying
directly to God
through the wall.
Praying to God,
through a wall.
A wall.
Prayers of lament.
Prayers of hope.
Prayers of wailing.
And here, the people cry out to God.
But speak into a wall.

Veni. Veni. Emmanuel.

Gay Not War

You say I have been blessed
For all the talent God has invested in me
But these are not gifts
I tell you, these are the skills
I have acquired in war

My flourishing is political
The cut of my cheek, a rebellion
My prayers, a violation

I fight because I cannot exist without fighting
I would choose not to use this arsenal
Come, let us no longer be blessed
Let us instead live
A quiet life

Forever Club Q

(in honor of the lives lost in the Club Q shooting)

We come to dance
In six-inch stiletto heels
Hips in motion
Spinning as we ride the swell of a bass drum
Quaking the foundation of a culture
Built on the bones of children they call, "those people"

We come for the disco balls
Glitter makeup and butterfly lashes
Cheeks cut and high drawn eyebrows
We are painted for the gods
And they will see us even after they place black bags
over our heads
Telling us to hide our faces

We come to sing
After they beat us in the alleys for choosing to believe
Water from the Christ and whiskey on ice
Might do better than promises in healing the wounds
they give us
And the music we play
Brings grace to the fray and sews up the torn soul

We light candles
And remember when they came
Armed with stones to cleanse us of our "sin" even after
Love has been written on our skin in cherry bright
  lipstick
They cannot touch our fire
As the air of "this time" enflames it

They come with bullets
We come to dance

What Got You into Drag?

I'm sitting in front of a small vanity, refreshing my lips with a touch of red. Behind me is a bed with satin black sheets and an array of scattered dresses, stilettos, and other essentials I use when I don the persona of Luz De La Rica. Nearby are a couple of chairs. One is a vivid dark green that seems to beg for attention against a white wall. There's lighting equipment here and a window that is easily covered with curtains and sizable backdrops that roll down from the ceiling. Amanda, standing to my right, is taking test shots with an impressive looking camera. This room in her home serves as a small photography studio that she uses for her clients. Today, that includes me. The room isn't large, but I know that a good photographer can use any space to tell an amazing story.

"So, what got you into drag?" Amanda asks.

I pause mid lipstick stroke. It's the first time that I've been asked this question. I'm surprised by this realization. In the moment, I'm unsure if Amanda is making small talk or if she is genuinely curious. I find myself having a brief, but intense internal debate. How honest am I going to be, not with Amanda, but with myself?

I resume the application of my paint. Amanda continues to fumble with her camera. Then, I try to find a steady voice. "I do drag because I'm angry."

There it is. I said it out loud.

"I was a pastoring a new church in the Christian Reformed denomination. New churches in that denomination are overseen by older established churches. When I came out, the leaders or council overseeing my work threw me away and tried to discredit me. I was working in the inner city, leading a growing multicultural ministry, hailed as a dynamic preacher... But, when I told them I was gay, they tried to wipe me from their history. To pretend like I never was."

Sighing, I add. "And I tried to take my life."

We sit in the intimacy of my confession before I continue.

"After losing everything, including my income and a place to live, I eventually got a job as an executive director at a non-profit that was housed in a church on the north end of the city. That church is part of the Reformed Church of America. A different side of the same coin."

I don't know if I'm losing Amanda's interest or not. I'm staring at myself in the mirror and force myself to continue.

"The non-profit had a farm that provided food to neighborhood food pantries, supporting hundreds of families in need while creating jobs for teens. But the church ended the relationship with the non-profit, forcing us to move after I was hired. They said it was because they had theological differences with the decisions the organization had made.

"They were more interested in proving a theological point than they were in feeding the hungry and taking care of children."

I put down my makeup. In the mirror I see the crown I won a few months ago when I claimed the title of Ms. Allegan Pride during a drag competition in Allegan, Michigan. It sits among the rubble that is my clothes, among the pieces that are Luz De La Rica. Amanda gifted me a photoshoot after winning the competition.

There is silence in the room now. In my soul I'm begging anyone and everyone to understand that drag is my protest against the erasure of my struggle. This is my art in the face of destruction. This is a beautiful reckoning calling us all to be more human. A glittery revolution. A refusal to be invisible.

"You want them to see you. To make it so they can't look away" Amanda is looking at me now, solemn but smiling. She understands. Her camera is now ready. "Let's get started," she says.

Book Two:
Aire

Descended of the Queen

(The Night Caj Monet Put Me into Drag)

We become her
Mitochondrial Eve
She brushes glue into my eyebrows
Pressing hairs to my skin
Using magic powder
To make her daughter appear
This is the transformation
To disappear an ego
Vulnerability must be given
A true face

We are immaculate
Mother Mary tells me
Keep your tears
Martyrdom is ended
And your eyeliner has already been applied
Her spirit released
With pencils, brushes and paints
The girl they told me
Was too soft, too dainty
Can now uncross her legs

Break her wrist
Command her hips
Part her lips
Give birth

On the Vine

If Christ is the vine
And we are the branches
Then, who is to blame
For the sweetness of the fruit?

Bread of Heaven

I do a silly thing
When Mami tells me to feed the birds
She takes bread from the fridge
The few slices she says have gone bad
Mostly, I think, Mami likes the idea of sharing
I sneak on her shoes, the low white heels
She leaves by the side door
Then I walk in confidence to the backyard
Grind up the bread and throw it to the air
It is manna from heaven that falls at my feet
And we have wandered enough through the sand
Eat my children, eat and be satisfied
Share in the bounty of who I am

The Church Rebirth

This is the Sunday morning survivors club
A bunch of queerdos sitting at breakfast
Coffee. Bagels. Yogurt. and Bibles
Someone smells of cigarettes
Or maybe it's the toaster
It keeps making the breaker flip
When it does, no one is surprised
Instead we chuckle at circumstances
How did we land in this storefront delight?
Exposed. Wires. Burgundy carpet and choices

Yeah, there's no power now
But remember, the rent is cheap
Pull back the curtains
That's enough light to see
No one is right here
No one is wrong

Yes, we are the chosen
A bunch of rejects in love with a question
Several questions really
Can we sing a song?

Sure, Erin.
What if I don't believe anymore?
All good, Rae.
What is that ringing?
Goodness, Tony. Put your phone on vibrate
We're communing with God after all
What if Jesus loves me, just as I am?
Who knows?
Pass the butter please

The straight guy, brother, buddy, gay-friend lunch.

I thought of you while
driving south on the expressway
when I turned on my high beams
cause it was raining
and it was dark and, well…
I have astigmatism

sorry. what I'm trying to say is
I was thinking of you sitting
across from me
when we decided to have gyros
across the street from the mall
and you crossed your arms. across your diaphragm
doing that funny thing you do
holding yourself when you laugh
and then I reached across the table and we briefly
  held hands
when you told me your brother died

I guess I think of you. sometimes
and by sometimes I mean. frequently
and by that I mean. everyday?

usually in the morning
specifically at 10:37am
that's when my neighbors jog past my house.
they're a couple. married I mean
they both wear these hideous neon green trainers
that's when you run through my mind
bad joke. whatever.
but we're not a couple. that's not what –

look. I always want to impress you
because you know trivia and books
you know history. dates and facts. kings and queens
and I. well, I like drag queens. oh, I like books too!
  and shoes
you like shoes too, I guess. from Goodwill.
and now we laugh! about your thrifty shopping
because you're thrifty and you're so cool about it! and
  I'm afraid
that most guys are afraid that when I say I love you.
  they think I want to…
well, you know. but not you. you just want to
ride shotgun in the car when it's time to get eats
and that makes it perfect

just two guys on the road together
I think about that. I think about that.

Enigma

We are in a sunken trench
Legs crossed, sitting in shiva
Heads tilted back to drink air

Christ in the void with us
We will surrender our doubts to death

Christ in the void with us
We will return to ceremony

Respond

You wait for the music to reverberate
Before allowing yourself to respond

But grace is enough and
External music is not the call to worship

Open yourselves to the trembling
Your lungs. Your arteries. The bass of your heart.
Now discover your voice
Find that your body is
The instrument

Photo credit: Hwa Jeen Na

I Wish It Was True

They said I would feel empty after I did it
And I want it to be true

I wish I felt empty
After I kissed this man
I wish I felt my soul
Shaking my holy temple
Crying out to God for salvation
I wish I felt the screaming
Laughter of demons
Wisping through my bones
I wish I felt Satan's hand
Dragging me by my tongue
Into the abyss of Sheol

But my soul, with a kiss, rejoices
I feel full of spring
Like dandelion seeds floating
Through the first weekend of May
I feel like the Messiah has arrived
He and I have been born again
Into a life without conclusions

I feel like I have been created
For something greater than Sunday
And it's morning hour of accusations

I kiss this man and I feel
The earth spinning
At the rate of majesty

I wish what they said was true
Because now I must ask aloud
What other lies have they told me?

Dandelions Are Edible

With a puff
I send dandelion seeds
Floating across the front lawn
The same lawn my dad is mowing
As he always does, in the heat of the day
At the worst hour for the grass

He yells at me for spreading weeds
Across the American dream
I can barely hear him
The SUVs and minivans
Of Burton Street don't care
About the sailing seeds
Our yellow dry lawn
Or the realization I just made

The joy of parachute seeds
Are the future weeds
In someone's lawn

All I want is a moment
To twirl with them like aerial acrobats
And bend the earth with a kiss of air

Who will teach us
In a world of manicured lawns
Dandelions are edible

I Am Not Your Enemy

Tropical eyeshadow palettes
Spilled silver glitter
Cocoa brown powder
A single purple glue stick and
This tube of mascara

Is this what you're afraid of?

Here, I'm taking off my skirt
Here, I'm storing my brushes in this briefcase
Here, I'm wiping off my makeup with
Disposable wipes and collecting them
For you to ask yourself why

Are you so easily fooled?
These things are easily packed
Quickly tossed away as refuse
They may disappear but
Your anger will still whisk
Your anger will
Bake

My drag is not the ingredient
Of what has bubbled in your marrow
What you taste is the fear
Of your unraveling veins
Telling you the truth

What they told you to hoard
What they told you to dream
What they told you to become
Was built on control

You have followed the rules
You have followed the map
You have followed their plan
You are now nowhere

Nowhere is where I am

The distance between us does not exist

Cross the chasm of lies
On this side, you will have
Less anger, less fear
You will have much more joy

Unrehearsed

My therapist asks me
So what is keeping you from doing it again?

No sermon
No catechism

No forced allofeeding
Of seminary professors

Give me
The answer

Here is where
Dispensationalism falters

Here is where
Calvinism hits a five point fail

Because the answer
The right answer is far too simple

No need to rehearse the formation
These syllables form in my mouth

I want to live

You Will Rise

Although you have set
Though you suffer through the night
You are yet the sun

The Trade Route

I don't belong here

I watch the sails of the ship catch the wind
The mast is greedy, like a bare arm
Reaching for clouds that never descend

I don't belong here

My own arms are bound, and white men are screaming
It seems they are threatening to throw me into the Ocean Sea
I have seen it before, and I have heard my people scream for mercy
Human bodies treated like commodities to be managed, drowning, murdered

I don't belong here

I reclaim myself and jump into that salty wind
My breath is gone, their ship is gone, my home is gone
To ease the conscience, I will be placed in the section
  of your history called
Ungrateful, unfortunate, ghetto child, at-risk-youth
Gangster, bottom feeder, rioter, unwilling participant
  in democracy
The result of Black-on-Black crime

I don't belong here

Hosanna on the Avenue

We stand on the sidewalk pondering our next move
My two white seminary classmates having just been interrogated
The owner of the bodega refuses to believe
They are Christians
La migra he says

I offer no immediate solutions. Instead
I take in the heartbeat of the Roosevelt Park neighborhood
The Spanish boom of cars pounding reggaeton through their stereos
The jingle of *el paletero* pushing his cart across the street
Friends calling *saludos* to one another

Grandville Avenue
The city now calls it, Cesar Chavez Way

Our class assignment. Write a plan to start a church
Our focus group. The Latin-American community
The target. Me

Selah

There are enough churches on this strip already
Jesús arrived on his donkey long before us
And it feels like we're here to collect the remaining
Palm branches trodden and a people already saved

I feel so out of place! Says my peer, shaking her head
Brings me back from hosanna to our present task
Now you know how I feel every day. I reply
We pause. The street continues
I turn back to praise

Here, in Heaven

I can see the end of all things
On the northeast side of nowhere
Heaven, on Sweet Street
From my front porch
Hanging flower baskets dangle
Sticky summer's kiss
Iced tea and lemonade
Large plastic chairs in the shade

The casualty of war is always children
But war does not reside
Here on Sweet Street
Here in the forever
Here the children catch footballs and
Shoot hoops on the empty tar road
Skip rope to new songs
Every one of them will grow old
Die and live again

Here my neighbor is not afraid
To wave, drop by, pet my dog
He's not afraid to take a seat
Hold my hand, share his favorite memories
Or sit in silence, for human company
Watch the sky become a kaleidoscope
Forget his gun and even fall asleep

Good Morning, Villa Mella

We still laugh about it, two decades later
Suffocating in the heat of Villa Mella
Roosters greeting the daylight
Mopeds and *motos* tearing through the strip road
Over the sound of an undeclared battle
Competing stereos of the homes nearby
Salsa, merengue, bachata, rap
Songs of lost love, lust, and for some reason a *burro*
Creating a cacophony that can disturb the mind
Of any Midwest raised girl, even if she is
Dominican at heart
All this at 8am.

Sanity is erased when the neighbor lady begins to sing
But is it singing? When the notes clash with the entire *barrio*
She sounds like the war cry of the four horsemen of the apocalypse
Even if this is the second coming of Jesus
My second oldest sister has had enough
Hair in a bedhead afro, she flings off her covers
Pulls open the wooden window shutters of our room

Screaming, SHUT UP!
SHUUUUT UUUUP!
SHUUUUT UUUUP!
And of course, no one does.

Instead my sisters and I join the confusion
The three of us in our in our pajamas, howling with
laughter
At the absurdity of songs about donkeys
That a woman can manage to screech
Louder than her boombox a full volume
About screaming in English when no one can hear you
And no one understands
Knowing that this will be our entire summer
Giggling with tears rolling down our morning faces
Until we're called to a breakfast of bread and coffee

The Pax

Oh, humble lamb.

In a world where violence is the law,
In countries where people are abused by corruption
  and theft,
In cities where the poor are ignored,
In neighborhoods shaped by oppression and prejudice,
In homes where brokenness abides,
In hearts full of doubt and strife,
Set up your throne and establish a kingdom of peace.

And let it take hold in me.

Photo credit: Amanda Adams

Voice

It is a drop of water making the softest ripple in the
stillest pond
It is a waterfall boiling at the source of life
It is your best friend whispering in your ear about
their secret crush
It is the end of a reverberating scream
It is the puff of air you've waited for on a humid
summer day
It is the raging wind of winter blanketing the night
It is an operatic soprano in full regalia
It is the deepest end of a belly base
It is the planting of marigold seeds in the soft dirt
It is the shaking of mountains from their ancient homes

It is the voice of God that calls me

I am called to live
I am called to glory

Home

I wonder what it's like to come home
To be welcomed into a place
Where your body matches your spirit

What would it be like? To find
The front door unlocked

You approach and the port eddies open
The whoops and applause greet you
The final sibling has arrived
Here they all know that you
Fell off your bike at six-years-old
Scarred up your knee
They know about your first crush
Your last crush
Your first kiss
Your favorite color
The warmth of orange

Might it be a delight?
They tease you a bit
Nothing serious

Ruffle your hair
You laugh and don't care
They invite you to share
A game called
Remember when
Sister burned the pancakes
Summer picnics in the backyard
Snickering during church service
Playing hide and go seek
Counting down
Getting caught
And giggles of joy

I wonder what it's like
To have dinner together
You come to the table
It's your turn to pray
Yes, it's your turn
All are favored here
To lead the rest
Thanking the Creator for who y'all are
And what this place represents
Let us then, say grace

Matthew 6:26–30

He is the first man to bring me flowers
Chosen from the beauty of a backyard field
He dresses with care, orange button down shirt
His brown beard, generous flecks of gray
His thin lips curve into a smile

We meet at his favorite coffee shop
Just east of the intersection
Diamond Avenue and Wealthy Street
No shame, open exchange
At a place called Sparrows

It's what I've always wanted
Flowers, coffee, and the freedom to touch
Chairs at a square table
The simple pleasure of a conversation
Nothing is broken, nothing is healed
And for an hour, God holds my worries

We Talk to Monsters

We talk to monsters
When the afternoon light is still good
Making home for us on this side
Of sliding glass doors

We sit on the couch
With the monsters
You and I holding hands
I find the wonder of an Arizona sky in your eyes
You find the earth in mine.
And we make friends with the air between us

These monsters have become our friends
The past has brought us
The pain has taught us
This fear has caught us
And they sit around us
Reminiscing on the adventures that we've had

A beater car abandoned
Thirsty treasure hunts
Laughing with those that left us behind
Regrets that we've slept with longer than they deserved

The monsters. They love us
They want to stay. Forever. But they know
A midwestern goodbye. Bye… Bye.
Finally, we send them along with to-go containers of
  leftover cheesecake
Thank you, we say, for being a friend. A hearty laugh.
  And we know
We'll see them again. Soon. Maybe next week

And then. It's just us
A few hours older. Several pounds heavier
Are you still sober?

You pour the wine
I slide the doors to the deck open
We close our eyes and breathe
The fading of the sun

Red Winged Blackbird

My favorite is the trill
The summer song of the red winged blackbird
That flutters between the cattails of the swamp

This place is so full of dead things
Crispy leaves and muddy water
Bleached white tree trunks that reach
High against a blue sky
With no arms but just a body of praise

It's so beautiful here, among the dead things
If you just stand still and smell the earth
Hear the chirping of crickets and frogs
Taste the sun and wind
Burn and cool your skin

The red winged blackbird takes it
Home without permission
Joy among the reeds

When it's all over
I think I'll come back here
I'll be the red winged blackbird
Not for God, but for me

Into the Mist

Someday this summer
I will cross through a mist
Gravity will release my burdens
And I will float, just for a second
Just enough to make it through the rainbow
The spectrum of color for the chosen ones
The vision of the unlikely

It's the country of the lost
On that side of the rain
The land flows with milk and honey
Promises are unspoken
And the unwanted drink freedom wine
From grape vines large and plentiful
There will be room for me there

Aire

Amanecí con tu nombre en mis labios
Poesía en mis pulmones
Lenguaje en mi boca

Por la primera vez en este vacío
Creo en el elemento

Aire

Air

I woke up with your name on my lips
Poetry in my lungs
Language in my mouth

For the first time in this void
I believe in the element

Air

Worship Interrupted

"Will you pray for me?" she asks. "I'm 'coming out' to my parents tonight, and I need the right words and the courage."

We are in the middle of our Sunday evening church service when one of my ministry volunteers introduces me to this young woman. There are singers on stage leading the congregation in worship with a keyboard, guitar, and several microphones, so when the volunteer tells me this young woman's name, I miss it. It's hard enough to hear her prayer request over the music. We are in the Burton Heights neighborhood, in a storefront building that has been converted into an alternative-style sanctuary. The walls are painted black and there is a large stage area opposite the main street entrance to the building, also colored black. It feels more like a black box theater than a temple, but it is sacred, nonetheless. And it's the best we could find for our start-up ministry, En Vivo Church, which I launched with a handful of leaders just a couple of months ago. The space we're renting belongs to a charismatic church group, while En Vivo Church belongs to the Christian Reformed Church of North America, a relatively small Christian denomination concentrated in cultural pockets of the United States and Canada.

The volunteer tells me in my ear, "She can't stay for the whole service. She's meeting her parents tonight."

The young woman is about 5'8". Her hair looks strawberry blond, and her eyes hold a timid, but resolute character behind a pair of round glasses. Her skin, already fair, looks even more so in the dim lighting of the room. She gently puts her hands in my own and closes her eyes, ready to receive whatever courage I can offer through the power of the Holy Spirit. I close my eyes with her and open my mouth to speak. Abruptly I feel like I have nothing to give. This is the third time someone openly identifying as gay has come to our church and I feel like a coward in the face of their search for hope.

For weeks I have been walking up and down the neighborhood along Division Avenue sharing the encouragement of the Gospel. The community is populated by Latin-American immigrants, not unlike my own family of origin. A former red-light district of Grand Rapids, Michigan, the street still holds the visible signs of decay including daytime drug deals and a boarded-up porn cinema. Occasionally you can hear gunfire in the night hours. None of these things bother me when I move into a loft apartment just south of the major intersection. I'm not even afraid when a dead body is found in the parking lot behind the apartment building. I grew up in this hood and I am ready to do God's work as the pastor of En Vivo Church. In my naivete I never imagined I'd be praying for someone to find the courage to tell their parents about their homosexual longings or sexual orientation. Nothing in my conservative Christian education prepared me for such an honest request.

The truth here is that I have nothing to offer the young woman because I have yet to find the courage to tell my own parents, "Mami. Papi. *Soy gay.*" Will I ever be able to tell my dad that I like men the way he likes mom? Will I ever be able to tell my mom that I used to parade around in her high heeled shoes, wishing that I could walk onto Burton Street like a glamazon taking the streets of Paris during fashion week?

I am gay.

I do my best to pray for God to lead the person before me because I certainly cannot. In the end, after my generic prayer, she gives me a warm smile and even hugs me. I watch her walk out of the sanctuary and back out to Burton Heights with all its glory. I wonder after she leaves, did I pray for her, or did I end up praying for myself?

That exchange of prayer and a hug changes the trajectory of my life. A short time after, on the other side of a dark night of the soul, I determine to no longer hide my sexual orientation from my parents, from my congregants, from my denomination, or from anyone else.

Book Three:
Lo Que Se Pierde

Passing

1. But he did die that morning
At thirty-two years old
One year younger than our Lord, Jesus Christ.

2. The modern apostles laid oily hands on his head
To pass on the power of the Holy Ghost
Leaving only phantoms to wander in his hair
A fog of questions that journeyed to his lips
How does it feel, knowing that you will be forgotten?
How does it feel, knowing that you were never known?
It was enough.

3. He crawled into the tomb
Waiting for the shivers of ending
Disappearing instead into a light
It came from behind him, through the blinds of his window
He became me, watching the steady stripes of morning
Emerging on the beige wall of my bedroom
The ritual of passing is done. And he is dead
There is no resurrection.

Same Block, Different Day

We felt so exclusive
We felt so grown
Though we had no money
But knowing that Mami would
Buy us Malta India
If we just ask

Stop at the Korean-owned bodega
On the way home
From the Spanish-speaking service
In the gym of Maplelawn Baptist Church

Los Coreanos, Mami calls it, at the time
Is the closest thing to a grocery store
I suppose the Piggly Wiggly isn't too far
Until it closed forever then
We're back at this grocery-like bodega
Always smells a bit like the fish
The cooler needs stronger refrigeration

Mami knows we need to keep summertime cool
Malta goes in her grocery basket

Con los viveres
Mami asks us which candy bar we'd like
At the register I see the owner's kid daughter
Looking back at me when I choose
A Zero candy bar
Mami always gets a Snickers

They never did replace the Piggly Wiggly
Not with a grocery store anyway
Some company took it over
The entire shopping center, when the Kmart closed
Twenty years later it still irks me when I drive by
On my way to my apartment that shares
A parking lot with the Korean-owned store
Los Coreanos, echoes every time I walk in

Exclusive is different kind of feeling now
When everything is too far away
When none of us get to travel that far
When I see the owner's daughter
Running the register, and I hope her dad is okay
When I can't really afford anything in here, or even
 my rent
Putting Malta India on the conveyor belt and a
 Snickers bar
They don't sell Zeros anymore

Downturn

It's a micro-economic tragedy
Church's Chicken off Franklin Street didn't make it
Could be because the Chicken Coop across the street
was here first
Even though you could casually scrape the oil off their
wall using your fingernails
Or could be because Popeye's was just down the way
Even though you could easily wait in line for a half
hour just for a three piece and a biscuit

As much as I love crispy fried wings, we didn't need
another chicken place here
The tragedy is that this corridor needs investments
Not placation

It's a spiritual crisis
Church's Chicken building has been taken over by an
iglesia pentecostal
Now we have a storefront charismatic movement just
north of Franklin
Across the street from two other storefront charismatic
startup *iglesias*

Now you have a chance to pray while you dodge
  homeless guys begging for change
All along the street are prayers to find the line for
  American citizenship

Because as much as we confess that Jesus paid it all,
  we still have bills to pay
The crisis is that we preach while this guy sleeps in
  the stoop of a storefront church

The workers give and the basket is always empty

Still Winter

Icicle fingers frame the window this morning
They remind me that this is January
Even if today is January 31st
It is January
Still

Blue and yellow quills of light wake the windowpane
They remind me that winter cannot kill the sun
Today the wind brings the air to 1° Fahrenheit
But we will have the sun
Still

Breaking inertia, I reach from my bed for my mobile phone. Missed call
It reminds me of who I am to a family of souls. Reverend
Today a life was collected from our remnant at 2:38am
And we are a remnant. Here
Still

Momentum crawls slowly for a Tuesday
The furnace nudges a cold draft across wooden floorboards
The dog emerging from the pillows, yawns
She nestles her neck underneath my arm
From here, I stare at the basket of clean laundry
Waiting patiently to be stowed
Knowing that that it will be ignored again
Debates on coffee, tears, sleep, and relief
Take their turns at the podium of my mind

The furnace. The wind
The ice. The light
The dog. The winter
The thoughts. This life
I remind myself that I am only a moment
A series of memories in formation
But only a moment
Still

What Is This Feeling?

I assumed that grief
Was always tied to an external body
One that gets entrenched in a cemetery
Or burned and collected in a polished box
Taking up visual residence
With the rest of the dust in the living room

No one told me
The decay you cannot see
Makes a dwelling called panic
You feel with every swallow
Daring you to weep in public
Make yourself the fool
So that over and over strangers ask
Where does this feeling come from?

How do you explain it?
No one died, but they killed you
You told them who you are and they left you
But not before taking all
Precious minerals from your vertebrae
Leaving you hunched

Don't Tell Me to Hush

You don't get to cut me
And then require your permission
To bleed or
Tell me when, where, and how loud
I can scream

This Conversation Is Over

Talking to you is emotionally expensive
It costs you nothing to listen
And costs me everything to cut
The diminished scars on my skin
Back, wide open, bleeding
Just to prove that I have trauma tissue
Surrounding my organs

It costs me too much
Just for you to make excuses
For Satan and systems
That don't need an advocate
Certainly not you verbalizing
Sticking out your tongue
From the side of your neck

Collective Trauma

They say that I am not well.
Because I am at Walmart
Paralyzed in the toilet paper isle
Weeping as I consider
That this is the end of humanity
There is not enough for all of us
To be clean and satisfied
Long after the pandemic of 2020 has passed
And just before the guns go off
In the halls of my local K-8

They say that I am not well.
Only because they hear me
Screaming out in public
About the urban deer eating the lettuce
At my urban farm
While I stand in line
At the downtown café
Behind this woman in a flower print dress
She's at the counter asking for milk alternatives
For her tea

They say that I am not well.
When they hear me cry for him
The man who gives seed to the birds
And sits alone every morning
Finding his peace in the absence of us
Because I just want to be near him
To feed the cardinals and have a moment
Flitter away into the safety of the sky
Where no one calls the police
Just for wanting to fly

April 13, 2022

(following the release of the video of the murder of Patrick Lyoya by Officer Schurr)

On this day in Black history
I put my armor on
Wondering how fast I'll need to run
How will I be considered if
I wear anything but a suit?
A clergy collar?
A tie?

How will I look?
The camera catching me
Running toward Breonna Taylor Way
Catching flames
Or running north on Division Ave.
Catching the rapid bus home

This is the city of Grand Rapids,
Where only the river runs undisturbed
After it's been stripped of its natural flow
I suppose it doesn't matter what I wear
In a city where this Afro-Latino will never be taken
seriously

Running to catch the urban myth of safety
In compliance I wear
A black t-shirt. Gray pants.
Say what you want. I wear my running shoes.

Supplication for the Queer Children

We pray for the children
The ones that who are taunted, bullied, and beat
When school boards tell them
When commissions tell them
When churches tell them
Speak the truth, but hide your colors

We pray for the children
For being wise enough to know who they are
And honest enough to say it out loud
Though no one listens
Though they know
Though they know

We pray for the children
Unbound by limits of adult imagination
For they are heirs to a kingdom not our own
They sing, every stone
Invisible but real
So bright and real

And we pray
Humbly, we pray
Have mercy, dear Lord
On each one of them
On each one here
And please
Let a little child lead us

Photo credit: Rebecca A. Dexter

Tu Política No Es Mi Seguridad

Tú eliges la neutralidad
Sabiendo que el otro lado me quiere muerto

Tienes la audacia de pedirme paciencia
Mientras averiguas qué es lo sigue
Mientras los veo afilar sus cuchillos

Your Politics Are Not My Safety

You choose neutrality
Knowing the other side wants me dead

You have the audacity to ask for my patience
While you figure out what is next
While I watch them sharpen their knives

Memorial

Like one hundred pounds of concrete
I am always in a cold dream
I am always in a cold prison
I am always in a petrified body

When did I become a sculpture?
Moss collecting in my nooks and shadows
When did I become history left outdoors?
A statue on the pavement we circumvent
The ignored reminder of what we all have done

Darkness Falls

And when darkness falls
I feel the blessing of your weight
Taking its place
On my naked torso
Giving new life to my lungs

You lean into me
Your fingers tracing
My eyebrows
And I lightly chuckle
Noticing you chewed
Your fingernails again

I reach for you
Aiming for the familiar
Weaving of our fingers
Giving them
Giving us
Permission

And now I'm gasping
Waking to find
Only myself,
Air and vapor,
Sunbeams and
Heavy drops of sweat

The Search Continues

I found a man to replace you
Same age. Tad younger
Same height. Stands taller
Same hair. Not the same gray
Same eyes. A paler blue
Similar lips. Much heavier kisses
Same build though
Just, not your dimpled behind
Not the same… you know
No one has it like you
He wears trainers
I miss watching you slip into your slip-ons
Stupidly miss your toes
Reminds me of you
He's nothing like you
Nothing like you

A Suitable Mate Could Not Be Found

On the sixth day
I learned that truth is an ideal
Most men only aspire to
But hope to never attain
Better to pretend to be whole
Than to admit they're missing a rib

The Last Time We Met

His lips are lush, but firm
Enough to imprint a memory
A kiss in the parking lot

His is a kiss that says
I'm about to climb into
My electric blue, European car
I don't need you

His is a kiss that says
I'm still in love with someone
My past.
I'm gay, and too old for this
My present.
And I chose to die alone
My future.

His is a kiss that says
We can't be friends
But call me anyway, for lunch

The Question

You press so insistently for the answer
Stripping the question of its dignity
You are afraid it will unravel your identity

The question cannot be contained by your insecurities
Anymore than God can be contained in a church

What We Never Said

Here are the signs that I know that you know

We always sat together in the front row at church
And now you say, do you have to sit here?

You taught me how to preach
And now you say, don't talk to me right now

We had ice cream, cobbler, and uno games at your house every week
And now you say, you are not my child

You called me disgusting
And sadly, now I can say that I understand

We could have said it differently
The rumors are true or
I'm disappointed or
Wow, I really expected you to be different

But you said disgusting
I said goodbye

The Loneliest Place

It's not where you don't have
Another to share in your sorrow
It's where you have not a soul
To share in your joy

Boy No Swim

I was never taught to swim
No one ever even bothered to
Toss me in the shallows
The irony of island blood
Drawn to the water
Unsatisfied

The pool at Garfield Park
Only two blocks
Away from my childhood
My family might as well been
Back in Fort Smith, Arkansas
Looking for the beaches of
Puerto Plata

We finally map it out
Drive to a free Lake Michigan
On the Fourth of July
When the inland silver sea waves
Hold me sweetly captive
I know I'll come back
Every year
And sink to the bottom
Every summer

Taking His Seat

He moves
Aiming for his favorite recliner

I'm watching television
It's my favorite show tonight

He moves
Now I'm watching him
And I see it's not the first time
He's slowing down

No more driving the bus until retirement
No more late nights writing sermons

No more power
No more yelling

Only fear. For me

I should say something. What can I say?

Papi?
¿Qué estás mirando?
Nothing. What do you want to see?

I hand him the remote

Gay Pastors Not Welcome

The Reformed church takes it back
My designated office space
A broom closet. Half a desk reserved for my use
Takes my nameplate off the door
Something about their values

The secretary brings the silver plate to me
Downstairs to the back door
Heading to my car she asks if I want to keep it
Half-smile on her lips

No, I reply
I'll remember who I am just fine
Without your flimsy things

It's Over

We end friendships through text messages now
I would rather you call me a garbage person, in-person
Than to read, best of luck with your lifestyle ttyl

Danos Este Día

Sal

No estoy abandonado
Aunque no puedo
Recordar cómo orar
Cuando tengo hambre
Cuando estoy débil
Cuando estoy sudando

Harina

No mendigo por pan,
Pero a Dios pido
Por la satisfacción de la justicia
Con los gemidos de mi vientre

Levadura

Se dará fuerza
Este no será mi fin
Este no será tu fin
Sé generoso. Presta libremente
Heredaremos este campo
Y lo habitaremos
Para siempre

Agua

Photo credit: Alfield Reeves

Give Us This Day

Salt

I am not forsaken
Though I cannot
Remember how to pray
When I am starving
When I am weak
When I am sweating

Flour

I beg not for bread
But from God I ask
For the satisfaction of justice
Through the wailing of my belly

Yeast

Strength shall be given
This will not be the end of me
This will not be the end of you
Be generous. Lend freely
We will inherit this field
And dwell it in
Forevermore

Water

Burning

"¡Pégale fuego a ese hombre!"

These are the words my father shouts from his window as he drives our rusting Suzuki pick-up truck to our storefront church.

It's Sunday morning. My sisters have dawdled in getting primped for service. My tia and Abuelita depend on us to get a lift to church, and they run perpetually on Latina time too. Papi isn't having it today. Since I am ready to go in my creased black pants and shoes. He tells me to get in the passenger side of the truck. He's leaving the women to their own devices. Mami will show up in her minivan eventually, all the ladies in tow, and I'm sure Papi will be fuming because they'll most definitely be late. As a family, it's our unspoken job to set an example for the rest of the church. Tardiness does not uphold the proper standard.

Papi is never the most patient person, and much less so on Sunday mornings. He is the lead elder of the church. I describe our church as a Spanish-speaking, inner city, independent Brethren church plant. Brethren churches don't have pastors; they're governed by a body of elders. Functionally however, my dad is the pastor. He started the church, he holds the key to the building, always gets there first, fills the pulpit, and it seems that whenever anyone has a question or problem in our church community, they come to him for prayer and guidance.

In retrospect I wonder how much of the responsibility my father holds is because he somewhat successfully navigates the systems here in the United States and West Michigan. Our church is composed of individuals and families from a variety of Latin-American countries, and most of the adult church members are still learning the basics of the English language and doing their best to find their way through the country's immigration policies. Regardless, my family is still climbing its way to the coveted middle class along with the rest of them. Collectively, we are the church called Asamblea Evangelica.

Even at the age of eleven or twelve, I'm reasonably sure that the building our church rents for worship stands in one of the most disenfranchised areas of Grand Rapids in the mid-nineties. I'm less sure on how the property owner gets away without making any desperately needed updates to the building. This is always evident in the colder months, when our small congregation gathers around a portable kerosene heater to keep warm because a functional furnace simply doesn't exist. But, where else can a start-up church of Latin-American immigrants and refugees afford to gather when its membership is composed of migrant farm hands and blue-collar workers? And so, my father drives a city bus during the week, and on evenings and weekends he preaches and teaches those who are new to faith. My job as his son and an able youth? Keep the fire in the kerosene heater running and manage it well so no gets burned.

I always internally collect the signs of hardship from our neighborhood and up Division Avenue as we head to worship. Boarded up buildings. Cars on lawns, hoods up. Refuse on the sidewalks. Ladies on the block corners who aren't waiting for the bus. A general sense of this is not enough. I'm collecting these visuals as usual when my father, with his window rolled down, shouts into the street. I'm caught off guard. "Light that man on fire!" He says in Spanish. I can't tell if he's joking or angry. What is he talking about?

I catch sight of a man on the opposite side of the street. At least he appears to be a man to my young eyes. This person is determinedly walking south on the sidewalk wearing a pink skirt, a crop top and high heels along with bright colored eyeshadow and lipstick.

Like with the neighborhood, I collect this image. I process it. A gay man is walking down the street and my father is telling the world to light him on fire. For the rest of the short ride, I'm also processing a secret. I have been sitting and holding it for what feels like all my life, though really I've only discovered it in the last year. I've never been sure of the best time to bring it up, that I'm not like the other boys at church or school. They talk about the hot girls and I pretend to be too Christian, too chaste to enter the discussion. I have to be the example. But the truth is my stomach stirs for guys and not for girls. I know what I am.

If I lacked the confidence to say anything about my attraction to men before, I am now terrified. Will people want to burn me too? We get to the church. Papi opens the door. There in the center of the room is the kerosene heater. I want to cry and ask, who will keep me from getting burned?

Book Four:

Cuerpos De Alabanza

The Epic of la Morena

Abuela sweeps her hair back
Ties it up
Soy fea. I am ugly.
She says.

Such a common refrain.

I watch her hands
Weathered, but unwrinkled
Her fingers chorus
A more ancient verse
Of waters pulled
By an invisible moon
Onto a sand formally known as
Unknown
Formally known as
Hispanola
Formally known as
Ayiti

These hands
They sing for days longer
Than her words
Of the epic called
Morena. Black.

We used to have
Good hair
Esta familia. This family.
She says.

Such an unusual instruction.

Stay out of the sun.
But the sun is where I play.

Marry a white woman.
But my sisters are *morenas*.

For your babies. For the hair.
But I delight in my waves.

She tries to erase herself
Powdering her chest
Her hands laugh at her
Controlled but undefeated
With the divine wrapped in all their color

As we go
They hold me.
When I cross the street
When we go to buy plantains
When we smash them. Fry them.
Guiding my cursive, when I learn to write.
And when I say my prayers
Searching for God.

Photo credit: Author

Cocoa Brown Girls

Part 1

These cocoa brown girls don't have money
Not for piano teachers honey
Much less, the best
Of them displaced
To this place
Called the Midwest

They're not white enough for that.

Caribbean separated, sun kiss
No one cares, that they miss
The flight, cultural height
New York to here
No one cares, again they hear
Go to school, learn to fight

When they discover,
They're not Black enough either
The world of rhyming ends.

Part 2

I watch them balance books on a nest
Wavy, nappy, curly black hair
Walk across the room with encyclopedias on their mind
Until they can do it with no pages falling open

I watch them do the impossible
Learn four languages at once
Spanish, English, Spanglish
And whatever the hell is spoken on the playground

Being separated by oceans and religion
From a place to belong
I watch them teach other girls
About the genocide called 1492
About how the diaspora is still displaced
About going from tragedy to identity
Never using words

No, not words because of a piano
Finding itself on a back porch
The cocoa brown girls taught themselves
To play the opening number of a TV show called *Cheers*
Openly aired, the neighborhood hears their progress

Cocoa brown girls teach themselves piano
On an unprotected instrument
Growing out of tune

Cubetas de Café

Ambos de mis abuelos
Agregaron un chin de leche
Pero mi sangre corre con
Cubetas de café
En ella nada mi ascendencia
Y mi corazón late negro
Tambores de cacao
Ritmo de resistencia
Dádiva de mis abuelas

El regresar a la isla
Triunfante
A una vida tranquila
Camioneta y campo
El sueñito de papi
Azúcar

Y los besitos de mami
La tasa
Acuérdate, hijo mío
Me dice, busca a Dios
Que los dones de esta vida

Alma y canto
Provienen del cielo
A nuestras manos

Buckets of Coffee

Both of my grandfathers
Added a little milk
But my blood still runs with
Buckets of coffee
In it swims my ancestry
And my heart beats black
Cocoa drums
Resistance rhythm
Gift of my grandmothers

To return to the island
Triumphant
To a tranquil life
Pickup truck and countryside
Daddy's little dream
Sugar

And mommy's little kisses
The cup
Remember, my son
She says, seek God
For the gifts of this life

Soul and song
Descend from heaven
Into our hands

Warfare

At 3:17am I give myself permission to heal
Spiritual warfare is released from my heart into my arteries
My nostrils flare, reclaiming oxygen for the beauty of holiness

The sinews of my muscles tie themselves together
My cartilage finds the capacity to regrow
Skin stretches like the membrane of a drum

At 6:34am I leave wrinkled sheets and sweats of blood
They lie crumpled just to the left of my mattress
My new flesh is chilled by the crisp touch of morning

Who Has Sinned?

No one has sinned
For us to be found in this state
We have been chosen
For the glory of God to be
Revealed

Wash the mud from your eyes
And see plainly
There is nothing wrong with you

Walk into the temple
Dressed in rainbows
And accusations
Let them ask, who let you in

Wink and say
It was the Nazarene

Girl, Be Sexy

Girl, be sexy
Or find me the Scripture
That says you have to look like a potato
To please God

Modest
Sure, whatever
But God gave you those hips
Gave you those lips
Tender, soft and juicy
And said that it was good
Girl, they are
Good

So maybe you should be
A temptation

Make a choice

Be a dare
For someone to consider
That maybe what God calls good
Is not for a man to decide

God made you those legs
All the way up made
Stand. Sit. Stretch them.

Rejoice in your own skin
It is not a sin
Again, and again
I say
Rejoice

Nice Shirt

It's like me complimenting your shirt
And you saying thanks and immediately
Telling me where you made the purchase
Telling me that you got it on sale
The way you always go to the clearance rack
And how much money you saved
The points you collected
Because you're a frequent customer
Instead of simply saying
Thank you
Just
Thank you

You are a phenomenon
And you do nothing for us
When you diminish your beauty

It's like you giving
All the excuses for why
You shouldn't be recognized
Welcomed to the table
Invited to the party

Given the award
Promoted
Exalted
Shine

False modesty is not for you
Be the badass
Queen

Recibe

No lo tienes que ganar
No tienes que probarte para esto
No hay ninguna escalera para subir
Ni una para que yo descienda
No protestes
Sólo extiende tus manos
Yo te creé
Y yo te amo

Receive

You do not have to earn it
You do not have to prove yourself for it
There is no ladder for you to climb
Nor one for me to descend
Do not protest
Just hold out your hands
I created you
And I love you

We Dance Naked

There is a time to mourn
a time to dance
and we dance naked

The ballad of dead things has played
it's final notes
we leave it buried
somewhere between the street and the door
the same with our clothes
somewhere

Here, in this sanctuary, we sway
our chests meet to house one heart beating
in skin and free
our feet step together a silent rhythm
toes lightly gripping the carpet
no one leads, we both follow
we sway, we sway, we sway
two regal men in the song of God's kingdom

Drag Queen Preacher

I meet a former sex worker in the dressing room
She's new to the city. Latina
We build a rapport together
Over our Latina-in-West-Michigan experience
To my left is a queen that worked in human resources
Until she got let go. She speaks up against bigotry
She's got a loud voice and a commands respect
Behind me a performer bares his breasts while changing attire
He speaks freely of transitioning, meaning
His story is still being written
And he's not ashamed of his destiny
Over there, that girl is a therapist
As in, she has real degrees and a day job
Okay, honey! Work it. And get me a referral
That young queen is new, searching for a mother
A seasoned queen that has been here for years
Helps the new girl adjust her wig
We all trade make up secrets and borrow hair pins
Laugh at the absurdity of
Nipples, sex, and family rejection
Excommunication

And it feels like church
Preparing to make a crowd of strangers feel
Invited into a place of belonging
To forget the pain of the world
For just an hour, yes, this is the church
And we are the preachers

Storytime Please

Please, will you tell me a story?

Of course, my darling.
Of a prince and frogs and fairies?

No, a different story.

Of course, my love.
Of princesses, dangers and dragons?

No, a different kind of story.

Of course, my child.
Of magic, swords and swans?

Of bravery yes, but no, mommy, no.

Tell me a story of losing friends.
Tell me a story where they don't always win.
Tell me a story where honesty doesn't always help.
Where it's okay to be lost.

Tell me a story of making new families.
Tell me a story where they just play.
Tell me a story where we don't have to prove anything.
Where it's okay to look like us.

Tell me a story that sounds like me.

Rest

Now is not the season
For seeding, weeding or harvest

This is not the week
To preach, teach, or even reach for another book

Nor is it the hour
For Wi-Fi connections, email ambitions, app notifications

And this is not the moment
For another chant, another sign, another picket line

No more sacrifices
You have given enough
And they should not have your body
As a tribute to their greed

No, this time
Count your wrinkles and your grays
Remember how you earned the scars
Feel the weight, the fight, they leave on your skin

No coffee today
Drink a glass of water
Drink orange juice and champagne
Go back to bed naked, the way you came

This is the sabbath
God says, let us rest

Advent

Pierce the veil
Enter a bed of flesh
Skin to skin
And breast to breast
Gather with me
This aching breath

Four hundred years
Of formless gasping
Empty grasping
Hovering over
The surface of the deep
Find room in this,
My quiet cave
Full of waiting night

Then, open your eyes
Let me cradle you
Behold you
Feel the change
Gentle and firm
Quivering and still

I am longing and whole
You are lovely and fierce
I take courage
You in my arms
God with us

Safe Now

Take me to your secret place

Steady the tremors between
Our intertwined fingers
And make room for laughter
When our eyes find company
With each other
The way we have laughed
In every lifetime

Unbutton your shirt
And I will walk through your ribcage
Cup your heart
Gently in my mouth

And now, we are one
I am no longer
You are no longer
A specter to endless waiting

Fear not
For I am with you

Beard Lust

It amuses me when a woman complains
About her husband's scratchy beard
I resist the urge to push her out of line
And dare that man to give his Susan a break
Please, sir, scratch up my face with your delicious bristles
Let me feel what it's like to live in the untamed

Can't Help It

I have a thing, as they say, for men with brown hair
who have gone old and gray

Russell Crowe
Jonathan Frakes
The white version of Jesus Christ

Baby, they turn my water into wine

Desnudo en la Ventana

Mi parte favorita es cuando
Él está desnudo en la ventana
Como si viera el horizonte por primera vez
Las sombras intentan ocultar las imperfecciones
En cambio, las capturo y las disfruto
Cada bolsillo de piel hundido. Cada hoyuelo. Cada
  línea
Me apresuro y lo abrazo por detrás

Naked at the Window

My favorite part is when
He stands naked at the window
As if seeing the horizon for the first time
Shadows try to conceal the imperfections
I capture them instead and relish them
Every sunken pocket of skin. Every dimple. Every line
I rush and hug him from behind

Photo credit: Amanda Adams

Preparing Face

I save my sideburns for last

Papi once told me
Las patillas for
A man is
What gives definition to his face
He was trimming my hair
And my innocence simply inquired
What if you cut off my sideburns today?

Today Papi isn't here
As I stand at the vanity
Of this bathroom mirror
And yet, he is watching me
I raise a razor. We smile
He might be right
And if sideburns define a man
Then they have to go

It's time for me to do my face

Breakfast in Bed

He is the satisfaction
Of strawberries in syrup
Thick. Warm. Pancakes
With just enough butter
To make him sweet
Cream

Familiar

Let me paint you
Beautiful
With the colors of music
The kind summer grass will hum
As it grows
When it first learns to whisper
Again come June

And don't run
As I paint
You will
Find me
Familiar

Familiar?
Yes, you see
I come not just
To kiss
Your lips
Your cheeks
Your hands
Your ears

More like breathing
Water and living
I come
To kiss
Your soul
Your smile
Your labor
Your intellect

To ignite a memory

Never to cover what is you
But yes, embrace you
Accentuate you
Any color
Can only prove you
To be
Beautiful

And always to bless
See through the curse
Sense the vibrations
Rippling
Emanating from your chest
And into my hand
Find us again

And I hope you will
Indeed
Find me

Oh,
To be
Familiar

Oh,
To be
Beautiful

Queer Psalm 23

Lord, let us rest
At the banks of this Grand River
In the greenery of this park
Refresh our weary muscles
From the beating we received at church
Just this morning

Though we have wandered
In the church pews
Hoping to find a scrap of welcome
We are lonely, but not alone
We are comforted by direction in the lost place
And in these shadows we find grace
For ourselves and other Queer travelers

A table is being made ready
We see it. They see it
A place of blessing right before
Those that wish to harm our bodies
Those that are afraid of losing power over us

Pour then the oil of your favor

Slather it across our gaping wounds
For in the name of the Shepherd Queen
Love will follow us
And I will be found in your presence
Forever. Now. Rest

Beautiful Are the Feet

The Gospel is carried forth
On black pumps
Bedazzled with stones
Announcing the coming of a new age
The poor shall receive increase
The prisoners shall be set free
All debts will be forgiven
Including student loans
During Sunday brunch
Arias will come through
Bluetooth speakers
Deliverance through praise dancers
In catsuits and sequins
Yes, this is the work of the Lord
Opening blinded eyes
Making the mute shout
Glory! For God is God
And we are not
To change who we are
To appease the will of men

Hello Sunday

Hello Sunday

It's okay for him to be gay they say
As long as he doesn't flaunt it
As long as he doesn't hold hands
With any man
In prayer
Or kiss
Anything but the good book

God loves you as you are they say in verse
Then turn to each other
The whispers that aren't whispers
Circulate the pews
The chorus of their hymn
Lists a dozen other things wrong with him
Just before they share communion
Hungry for a crucifixion

On the night that he was betrayed
Jesus took bread and broke it
But this is my body and not your bread I say

My attractiveness offends them with the good news
I carry in my eyes, my lips, and toes
And I go from the altar to the door
Shake the dust of my heels
And sing a raucous number for the world

The Lipstick Revolution

Receive the kiss of the Good Sis
The Holy Spirit
Then go and do likewise

Kiss the foreheads of the forgotten
Then pound the pavement
In a public place
Make it hold every bit of your weight

What did I say?
Strut through the eye of this needle
This urban valley is your runway
We, the revolutionaries, marked with a kiss
Follow behind as champions

Follow the Good Sis
Her name
Theirs
His and
Yours
Is Resilience

This Side of Glory

I wonder if I look foolish driving west on the I-96 highway from Lansing to Grand Rapids in full glam makeup and no wig. Well, it's kind of glam. My face looks decent, but I'm still a new drag queen emerging in my craft. At best, I appear to be a half man, half woman odyssey. I'm in a v-neck shirt exposing a bit of my chest hair and my mannish shoulders. My hands are locked in the ten and two position. The muscles between my fingers and neck are accentuated by the tight grip I have on my steering wheel. I haven't checked, but I must be doing at least eighty-five miles per hour trying to get to church on time. I can't help but imagine the gasps and the double takes of other drivers glancing up or peering at me as I zoom past in my red Ford Escape. I can hear it, the voice of some wide-eyed kid in the backseat of a vehicle calling to their mother, "Mommy, look. There's a clown driving that car," and the mother looking up just in time to see me and croak in shock.

"Whatever," is what I keep telling myself. "No one is looking at you and no one cares." I focus on being grateful that I was smart enough, for once in my life, to make sure I have enough gasoline in my vehicle before getting on the road. Imagining drivers pointing and laughing at me is one thing. Pumping gasoline as a man in hip pads and makeup in rural Michigan feels like putting my life in danger. "Whatever," I say again. "Lord, just get me there." I am set to appear for the first time at En Vivo Church's evening service in drag.

En Vivo Church has gone through significant changes since being dismissed from the Christian Reformed Church of North America for being Queer affirming. It is now a nomadic majority Queer congregation. Some of the church members have seen me perform in drag, but only our Worship Coordinator, Erin, is prepared to see me walk into worship this evening in my drag persona. I warned her ahead of time so she could properly introduce me before I step into the worship space, doing a lip sync routine to Kelly Clarkson's song, "People Like Us."

Worship at En Vivo has always been unconventional and more so now as a congregation of LGBTQ+ persons and allies. Worship must be untethered to tradition when the people in the sanctuary have traditionally been those sitting outside the temple gates begging for change. None of us at En Vivo Church had collected enough compassion at those gates. And yet, choosing to be unconventional and preach in drag at my church was not an overnight process. I knew the small congregation would support it. It would be an additional outward demonstration that anyone in the Queer community is welcome to worship with us. The hesitation doesn't come from anyone but me. I know that once I step into our makeshift sanctuary wearing my black stiletto heels, a part of my spiritual calling will be unlocked.

"Am I ready for this?"

I pull into the parking lot of a dying congregational church where En Vivo has found a temporary home for worship. With no official supporting denomination and limited resources we make home where we can. We meet every Sunday evening in this colonial style building in a space called the Drawing Room. It's a room that immediately reminds anyone who enters of a funeral parlor with its muted colors, drab furniture, and images of white Jesus. We aren't allowed to change the room, but it has a baby grand piano, which is nice, and En Vivo can't afford to go anywhere else. We would later learn that members of the congregational church were unhappy with a bunch of queers and a gay pastor using their facilities. Eventually, we would be unceremoniously disallowed from using their empty room as our gathering place. In this moment, however, it is as close to having stability as En Vivo can get. And as I turn off the ignition of my vehicle and reach for my dark brown wig, I think to myself, "I must have blanked out on the road. How did I even get here?"

Looking back to several years ago, I see myself leaning on my friend, Joseph, who had "retired" from the drag biz. Joseph and I met at Dog Story Theater as cast members in a production of *Jeffrey*. This gay-themed play ushers me, a recently uncloseted pastor, out of my proverbial comfort zone. The opening scene includes me materializing onstage in my underwear on a large bed, along with the rest of the cast. In that moment we portray the complexity of dating and sex for gay men in the presence of very real concerns related to HIV and AIDS in the early 90s, which is the context of the play itself. My role in the rest of the show is Sterling, an iconic gay silver fox with just the right amount of flair to make him sexy and admirable. I decided to use just a touch of foundation during the run of the show to capture the flawlessness of the character.

One evening during dress rehearsals, Joseph walks past the bathroom where I am getting ready with a bottle of foundation cream and a cheap makeup brush. With limited bathroom space available in the building, I leave the door open just in case anyone needs to politely kick me out so they can take care of more urgent business. Joseph, who is becoming a close friend, catches my eyes through the reflection in the mirror and kindly asks, "Do you plan to blend that foundation?"

"Blend? Girl, I don't even know what that means," is what I would have said if hadn't felt so embarrassed. I offer no verbal response. Joseph walks away. As a veteran of community theatre, I had been required to do stage-makeup in the past and I had to squash my fragile masculinity in the process. On the other side of the closet door, I admit to myself that I might enjoy using makeup, at least for the art of theatre. And I must admit that I need help.

At the next opportunity I invite Joseph to tell me more about "blending." And oh my God, who knew that a makeup sponge could do such magic. My basic makeup improves dramatically with his help. In the process I hear all about his life in drag, which piques my curiosity. He talks to me about pageants, gowns, nightclubs, fake boobs, and crowns. I wish I could feel as free as he did to display the feminine part of his soul in public.

Years later, when my interest in drag resurfaces, it comes in fury. The Christian-political quagmire of West Michigan didn't want an openly gay minister leading in the community development arena. I had to find a way to personally respond and free myself from a religious perspective that says you can only be of service to the world if you look and sound like a conservative evangelical Christian.

I am an artist. And what is art if not a resistance to conform? I returned to Joseph for tips and guidance on becoming a drag queen. I would become a living resistance.

I am nowhere near proficient in my drag presentation when I audition for a production of Kinky Boots at the Grand Rapids Civic Theatre. I walk in the audition room and aim high but am cast as an ensemble factory worker. I am still thrilled to be a part of such an important story, a musical that places drag as the centerpiece of love and acceptance on one of the largest stages in my hometown.

Here I meet Christopher, an illustrious drag queen who goes by Caj Monet and who takes the lead role of Lola for the production. It isn't until after the production closes and we've all returned our embellished red high-heeled boots to the costume room that Caj and I begin to really connect. I ask for a recommendation on purchasing a decent set of my own red boots and Caj begins to take me under her wing as a drag daughter.

It is at Caj's encouragement that I ended up in Lansing this afternoon. Caj had put me in full drag several months prior and showed me the part of myself that had been waiting to be discovered; I then took the initiative to appear in drag in public, including doing a few drag performances. The perfectionist in me, however, needed more practice with a professional. I told Caj about my plan to preach in drag this evening. My hope was to sit at her house and do my face with her nearby, so I could ask questions. Maybe I could get her to step in and save me from the anxiety of drawing in my eyebrows.

"Girl, no." says Caj, "I'm heading to do a private gig in Lansing. But why don't you come and get ready over there with me. The gig is a birthday thing at someone's house and I'm sure it will be fine for you to be there."

It turns out that the someone is a straight man who is celebrating his birthday by getting into drag himself, which was unexpected, but I decide to give my attention to applying my makeup and process that part of the experience later. The three of us are getting ready together, half naked, in a mirror so large that we all have room to spread out with palettes and brushes without being top of each other. I watch Caj apply her foundation, her powder, draw her eyebrows, apply her highlights, color, and blend it together in the right places. I try to keep up while imitating everything she does. At times I get stuck just watching her. "Do your own face!" she yells at me.

"God," I pray, "Just help me get this right."

Thankfully this old church has more than enough bathrooms for me to find one where I won't be disturbed. I step into the men's room on main floor, the door closes behind me, and I'm looking in a mirror not designed for someone trying to adjust a wig or appraise the proportions of the body I now carry. For a moment this is my world and I'm alone here. I put on a long button up blouse with a modern and artistic black and white design. If you look closely, you can see a face represented in the patterns. I leave it unbuttoned, and it drapes down to my calves. Everything else I wear is just plain black. But with the wig, damn if I don't look like a young version of my mother. I see an Afro-Latina smiling back at me when I look up for one final mirror check.

Finally, I say, "You look good, girl. Good enough."

There are many ways I could approach the Drawing Room without being seen, but I choose to walk through the vacant main sanctuary of the church. The pulpit and organ pipes are behind me as I make the middle path between the pews a promenade, my open blouse flowing as I strut and take a little spin.

I come out at the entrance to the main sanctuary. I can hear En Vivo Church singing worship music down the hall. The voices sound so lovely. I can pick out Erin's rich voice, and Scott, and Rachel… The congregational church has pictures of their pastors long dead on one of the walls in the foyer. I walk past this and other bits of history on display. I keep moving forward. The doors to the Drawing Room are open and I see my people sitting at plastic round tables, several of them with hands raised in worshipful exuberance.

Eventually the song comes to a close. I subtly make eye contact with Erin to let her know I'm here, to let her know I'm ready.

"We have a special someone here to deliver the message here tonight," I hear Erin say. "Give me a second while I get our Bluetooth speakers ready because she's entering with some special music…"

There is a pause. A breath.

"Alright, here we go," she says. I feel an opening in the fabric of spirit and body. "Please welcome, Reverend Luz De La Rica."

Index

Acknowledgments

This collection of poetry has been a work in progress for more than a couple of decades. As someone invested in the art of language, I know that a few pages are not enough to name everyone that has been a part of this journey, nor enough to capture the immense sense of appreciation I feel for those that have encouraged, nudged and sometimes pushed me toward completing this book. Thus, here I offer just a small picture of those to whom I owe a debt of gratitude.

To my parents, thank you for a foundation of faith. While we disagree on God's love of the gay community, I thank you for your commitment to raising your children to love God and neighbor, even in the face of much adversity. This part of my upbringing continues to shape my voice as a writer, minister and artist. And to my two older sisters, your perseverance as women of faith and creative souls in difficult times always inspires me.

To my Abuela Luz and Abuelita Lina, my writing and identity has been shaped by your legacies.

My sweet Tia Nidia, thank you for indulging me when I was a young boy. I told you I wanted to write a story about dinosaurs. You put a typewriter in front of me at your dining room table and I began to imagine myself as an author.

Mr. Larry Lang, you were my first, and one of my only Black male teachers. You kneeled to meet me eye to eye at my fifth-grade desk and told me I had the gift of gab and writing. This memory is ingrained in my consciousness forever. It was like telling me I could fly and then pushing me off a cliff. I've never been the same.

Mr. Amen Bow, you taught me how to use my wings when you introduced me to poetry. I know I wasn't the easiest student for you to manage your in seventh and eighth grade honors English class. You're resting in God's arms now. I wish I could have given you accolades before your departure.

Professor David Cope, your creative writing class at the community college was so good for me that I took it twice! The experience you shared was what I needed to soar. Becoming a writer was no longer a dream. You made it attainable.

En Vivo Church, thank you for supporting and suffering with me as we continue to create a new kind of worship experience, one that centers, affirms and celebrates people like us. And thanks for letting me use my love of writing and poetry in my sermons on a regular basis. Similarly, to the staff and board of New City Neighbors, thank you for following me as we pressed for full inclusivity of the LGBTQ+ community in our ministry. En Vivo Church and New City Neighbors, you granted me the sabbatical that made this this project possible.

To my Canadian "parents", Barry and Beth Fellinger, thank you for lending me cabin space when I needed to get away and regain my sense of direction. It was there that I disciplined myself to just keep writing until this book found life. I found my north star under your care.

To the Dog-Eared Café of Paris, Ontario, thank you. I was a traveling spirit who took up space on your red couch for nearly a month. When I dropped in desperate for coffee and Wi-Fi, I didn't know that I would be compiling a significant portion of my manuscript in your establishment. You held an open mic night and invited me to share some of my work. The audience response confirmed that I was on the right path.

Allan Greene, thanks for letting me put the final pages of the manuscript together while sitting on your couch. The company you offer is a treasure and the sass you deliver is a delight. I adore you.

Gimbiya Kettering, I love that we are connected as POC writers with a Brethern background. Thank you for being a sister and being the first person to read the draft of my manuscript. You said it was like drinking from a hose and that still makes me laugh. Your commentary was invaluable.

Rev. Shannon Jammal Hollemans, we were forced out from the Christian Reformed Church to find bigger skies.

When I told you I was working on a poetry manuscript reflective of my healing, you pointed me to Pilgrim Press. Thank you.

To the team at Pilgrim Press, thank you for receiving the sample of my writing and saying, "yes" with an incredibly quick turnaround. It has been a most affirming experience working with you. Katie Martin, you are the perfect editor-match for me. Thank you for asking hard questions, compelling me to do rewrites that sharpened my work, organizing the collection, keeping me disciplined, and giving me the gift of camaraderie as a fellow rebellious dancer.

Jason Nobbs, you always hold my hand. You always tell me I am worthy. You always remind me of the beauty of the world. You are the concert for my soul.

About the Author

Rev. R.R. Tavárez is the justice driven leader behind the drag persona of Luz De La Rica. Rev. Tavárez is the founding and senior pastor of En Vivo Church, a Queer-led and Queer-affirming ministry in the United Church of Christ. He is also the Executive Director of New City Neighbors, a non-profit that creates employment and leadership opportunities for teens through an urban farm and a farm-to-table café, which supplies fresh produce for neighbors and food resource centers. Both En Vivo Church and New City Neighbors are a part of the Creston Neighborhood of Grand Rapids, Michigan, where Rev. Tavárez resides. In addition to performing in drag, he is an actor and award-winning artist and photographer. He also enjoys singing with LanSINGout, an LGBTQ+ chorus in Lansing, Michigan. In his various areas of ministry and artistry, Rev. Tavárez invites us into considering different perspectives to create social awareness while also moving us toward self-acceptance and the practice of equity.